TWENTY YEARS ON

FOR

my wife
Marianne
and my children
Alice, Jane, Sophia and Charlie

also
David Bailey
who taught me
and
Barry Taylor
who has always been there for me

JOHN SWANNELL
TWENTY YEARS ON

FOREWORD BY
SIR BOB GELDOF

'Nothing in art should be chance, not even movement'

Degas

PAVILION

First published in Great Britain in 1996 by
PAVILION BOOKS LIMITED
26 Upper Ground, London SE1 9PD

Art direction and design by Grant Scott
The moral right of the author has been asserted

ISBN 1 85793 917 4 (hbk)
ISBN 1 85793 922 0 (pbk)

Typeset in Perpetua Titling and Stempel Garamond
Printed and bound in Italy by Conti Tipocolor

2 4 6 8 10 9 7 5 3

This book may be ordered by post direct from the publisher.
Please contact the Marketing Department
But try your bookshop first.

FOREWORD

When I was young and thought I could do nothing. I decided to be a photographer. It appeared you didn't do very much and you drove around in a sports car and shagged a lot of girls called Raybanna or something. I could do that. A sorry, short-term career ensued as assistant to a man whose principal contract was the artistic snapping of soft-porn magazine centrefolds.

Tired of tits, my £11 a week and a house rule which pertained to all – save the photographer himself – which forbade all physical contact with the pouting, spreadeagled lovelies, I was relieved of the burden of tendering my resignation only by the peremptory termination of my career upon ruining every single frame of the great man's first (and, so far as I am aware, only) big break into fashion. I've never heard of him since. Disillusioned, I turned elsewhere, and quite frankly viz. photography, it can be justifiably said that the Instamatic disposable may well have been invented with me in mind.

Given the direction in which my life did ultimately turn, I have also perforce been rather too frequently the object of that same machine's attentions, but from the pointy end this time. And it is true and strange that as my apathy towards the camera grew, my antipathy towards being its target increased commensurately. (Geldof's First Law of Photography can therefore state: it is axiomatic that the distinctive loathing and reluctance to having one's picture taken is in equal and direct proportion to the taking of pictures oneself.)

Twenty years ago, when it all began for me and John Swannell, I used to like having my picture taken. It seemed fun – all the posturing. Now I resent the time, the boredom, the inevitable result. The resignation that the camera has confirmed once again that one is indeed incredibly ugly. That yes, one's hair is indeed horrible and there is nothing one can do about any of it. One doesn't really register oneself in the mirror in the morning, but the problem of the photograph is that it makes you *look*. And I never like what I see. I don't *feel* that I look like that. I don't *feel* that's what I sound like . . . but I do.

I still look shite in John's pictures, and in the one here I think I'm thinking about 'how long is this going to take', but he makes me look moody, in deep thought. Not quite so idiotic as normal. In reality I'm probably singing 'Dancing Queen' or something in my head, but because of my floppy face and his skill, he makes recognizable someone a lot of people are familiar with and, unlike a snap, they recognize the 'idea they have of that person'. That's a photographer and it's an art. I don't know if it is something you can acquire. You can possibly be trained to take photographs but I'm not sure you can be taught to have 'an eye'. To see light and line, to frame an instant, and to seize its emotion for ever. That is surely innate.

I don't think you can say John Swannell 'began' twenty years ago. He was probably doing it intuitively in his head long before he held a camera. And the camera is only the device, the alchemical tool which transmutes mind, brain, eye and soul into a chemically fixed eternity. It is true that he learned a lot from his friend Bailey, and studied and spoke to the masters, and in this book there is often discernible homage. But I've had my picture taken by a lot of them and although it is still always the same droopy face, it is simultaneously different. John's picture of me is different from theirs. Why? It's the same person. It's very odd.

In the portrait, the photographer tries to find a 'something else', something fleeting but so intrinsically characteristic that the viewer will say that's a 'good portrait'. By that they mean they see fixed before them something they understand about the sitter. The very opposite is true of fashion – personality is anathema. The look is everything. The model must disengage, her personality must not subsume that of which her vacuity for hire is so well paid – the clothes. The clothes are made with an attitude in mind – not any particular person. The personality has been cut into the cloth and must be cut out of the picture. Swannell cut his teeth on this stuff and while, for me, fashion photos are the least interesting, John has transcended the style time-limit usually inherent in any fashion photo as a result of ephemeral trends by the incredibly simple technique of taking good photographs. The lighting is daring and stark. There is no clutter. No fussiness. The girls' faces are rooted by their hair and eyes – their look in their transient moment, but the photos, the unfussy light and line, fix them in the imperishable present.

When Swannell takes his models and puts them into the landscape it seems that they breathe again. Though they may simply adorn a rock or lie inexplicably at the foot of some monstrous ivy root, he has invested the picture with soul. It's not simply that the beauty of the body cancels the glory of Nature or that the primal sensousness of flesh moulded to the earth is beautiful and true, or simply that a nice arse walking up a country road towards a wood with fluffy clouds is somehow strangely frightening but sexy, it's that here, more than anywhere, you get a glimpse of a man who really loves taking photographs. You begin to get him.

I've known John a good while now and I know his work, but I was completely taken aback by his landscapes. I had no idea. I had never seen them. It was like Ansel Adams had decided to go to the Lake District on a walking holiday. Here were truly passionate pictures. Everything hinted at before – technique, clinical authority, mastery of form, assumed, assayed and real moments of passion coming together in this literally panoramic *tour de force*.

It had been a long time since I'd seen any landscape photography. Particularly British landscape photography. It's odd because British art and sensibility are so rooted in the rural. Our attempts to import the country into our cities, to our parks and suburban gardens is only equal to the Englishman's escapist dream of a 'place in the country'. Swannell is clearly a photographer in this tradition. I'm not sure he knows it yet, but on the evidence of these pictures he needs to get out there and bring back to us his vision of this country at millenium's end.

This, then, is his chosen selection of twenty years of looking. It must be hard to sum up a period that by definition transcends mere work. At the same time he could do so with a certain amount of quiet satisfaction. A self-congratulatory but modest nod in the 'not bad, John, not bad' direction is completely justified. The rest of us are left to look at ourselves or our surroundings or other people through a singular pair of eyes that has for twenty years stared unblinkingly around, always looking, and always with a sense of wonder.

Doesn't mean you're taking my picture again soon, though.

Bob Geldof, 1996

FA
SH
ION

LISA B 1994

MARIANNE LAH–SWANNELL   1981

IMAN 1985
OVERLEAF: AUDREY THOM 1986

MARIANNE LAH–SWANNELL 1980

WENDY HOWLAND 1977

IMAN 1984

HELEN HOWLAND 1988

ALICE GEE 1985
OVERLEAF: MARIANNE LAH–SWANNELL 1980

NICOLA CHARLES, JULIENNE DAVIES 1993

ABOVE: MARLEN KOEHLER   1996
CECILE THOMPSON   1994
OVERLEAF: MARIANNE LAH–SWANNELL   1980

SUSIE BICK 1986

IMAN 1984

GEORGIANA 1994

FRANCESCA   1983

KIM HARRIS 1978
OVERLEAF: MARIANNE LAH–SWANNELL 1982

DEBBIE MOORE AND LINDY CHRISTENSEN 1976

JOSEPHINE FLORENT 1978

N UD ES

PORTRAIT OF A GIRL 1978

NUDE
BENEATH TREE 1985

GIRL BY RADIATOR 1990
OVERLEAF: RECLINING NUDE 1990

BACK VIEW 1987
OVERLEAF: DOME SERIES NO. 2 1991

COUPLE ENTWINED 1991
OVERLEAF: NUDE AND ROCK 1995

NAKED VINE   1985
OVERLEAF:
NUDE BENDING OVER   1990

PREVIOUS PAGE NUDE, UTAH 1989
ROCK FACE 1991
OVERLEAF: DIAGONAL NUDE 1993

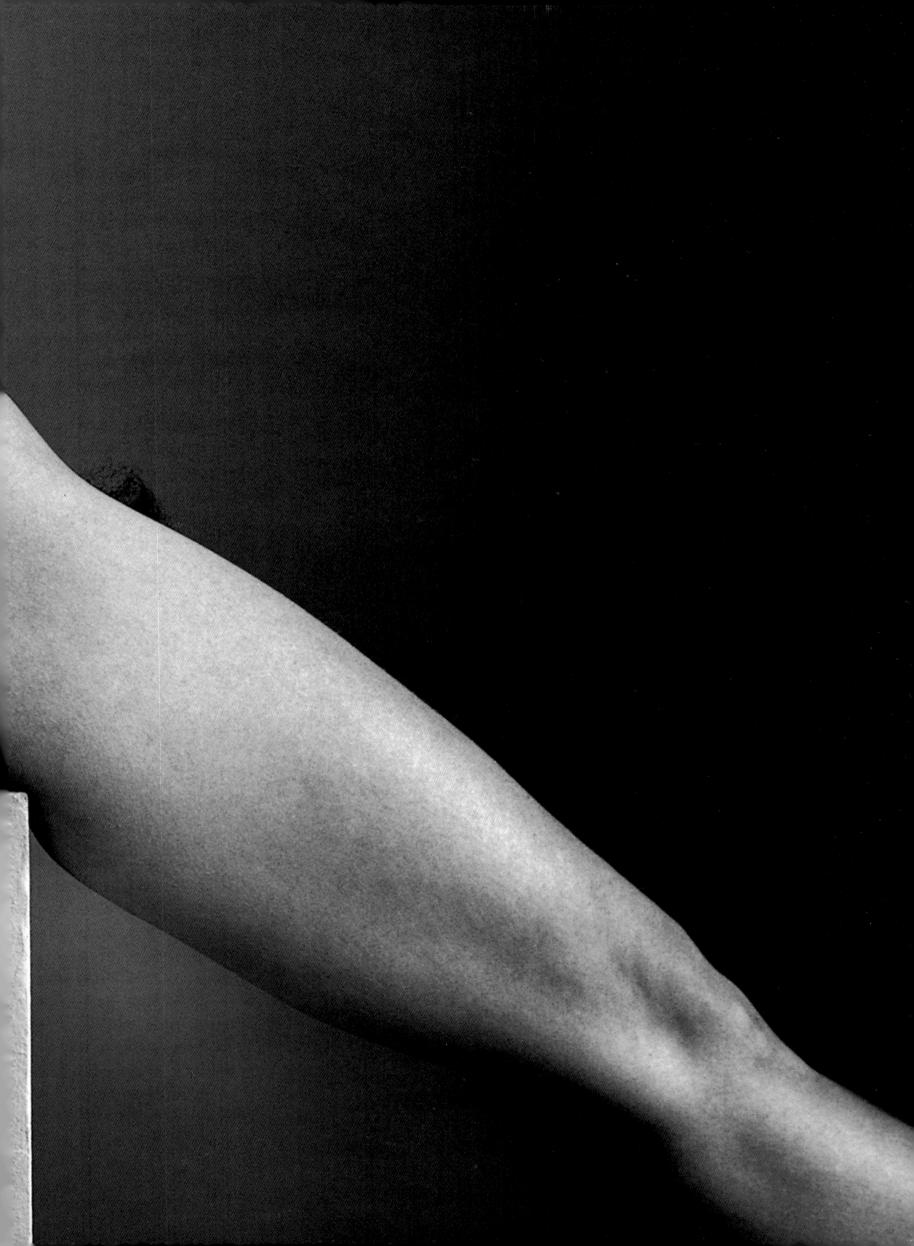

RODIN SERIES NOS. 1,2,3,4   1991

NUDE BY STREAM 1984

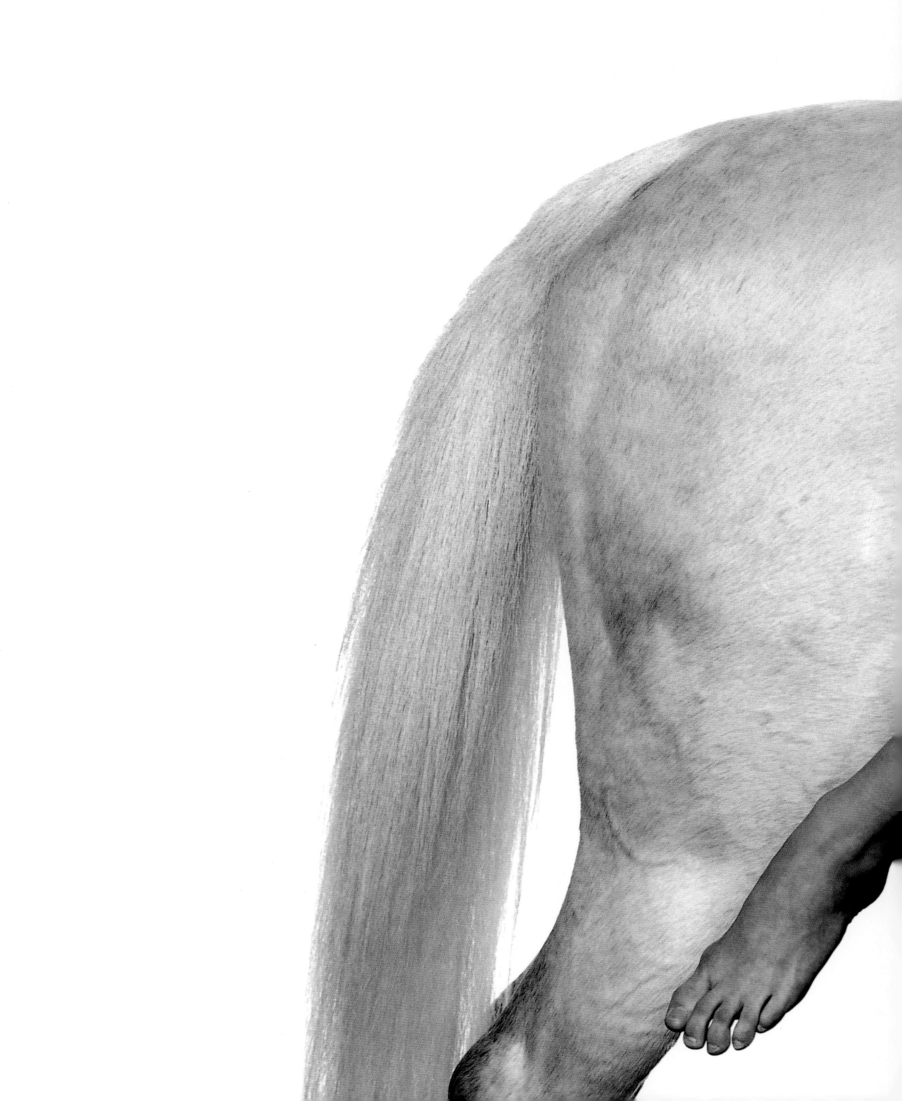

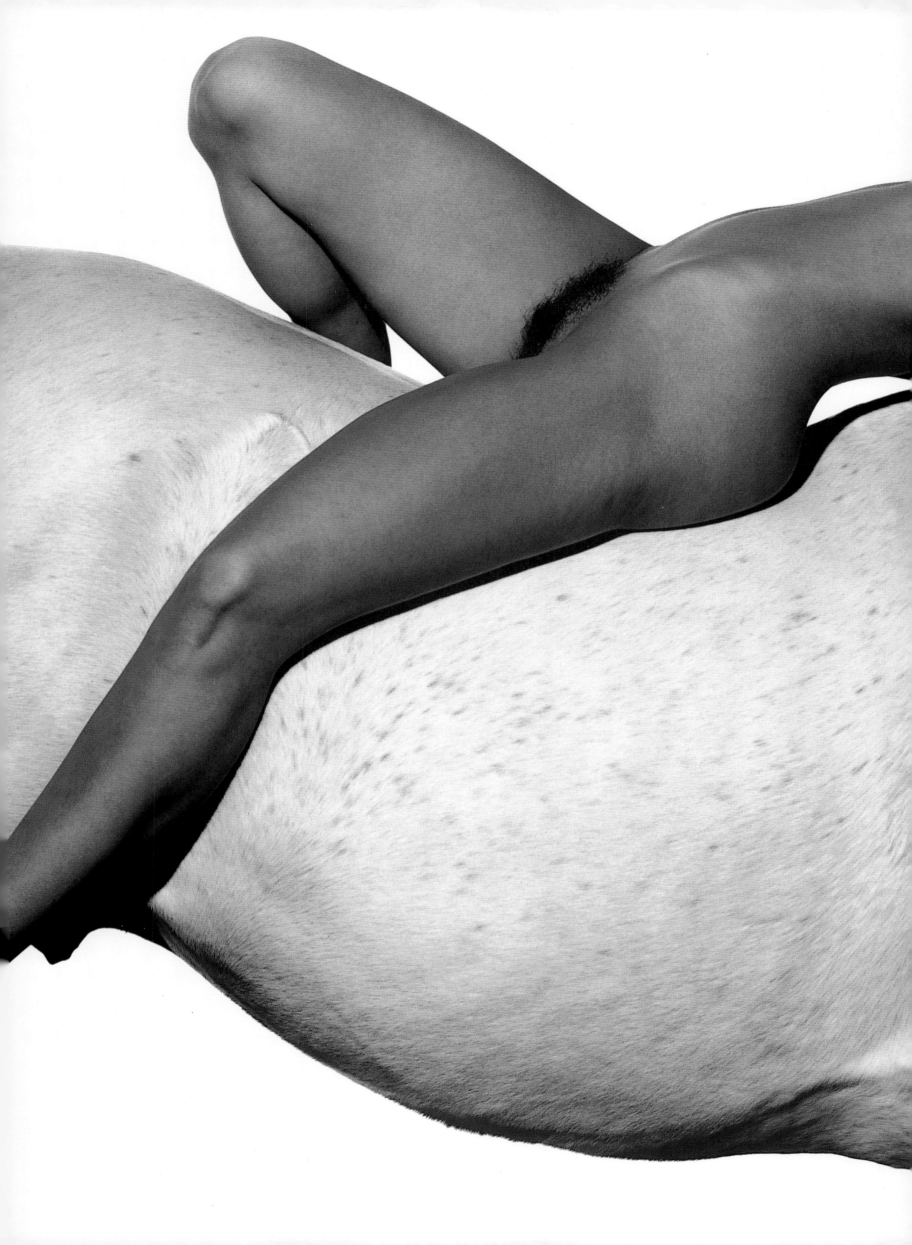

NUDE STRETCHING 1991

CHAIR SERIES NO.3   1991

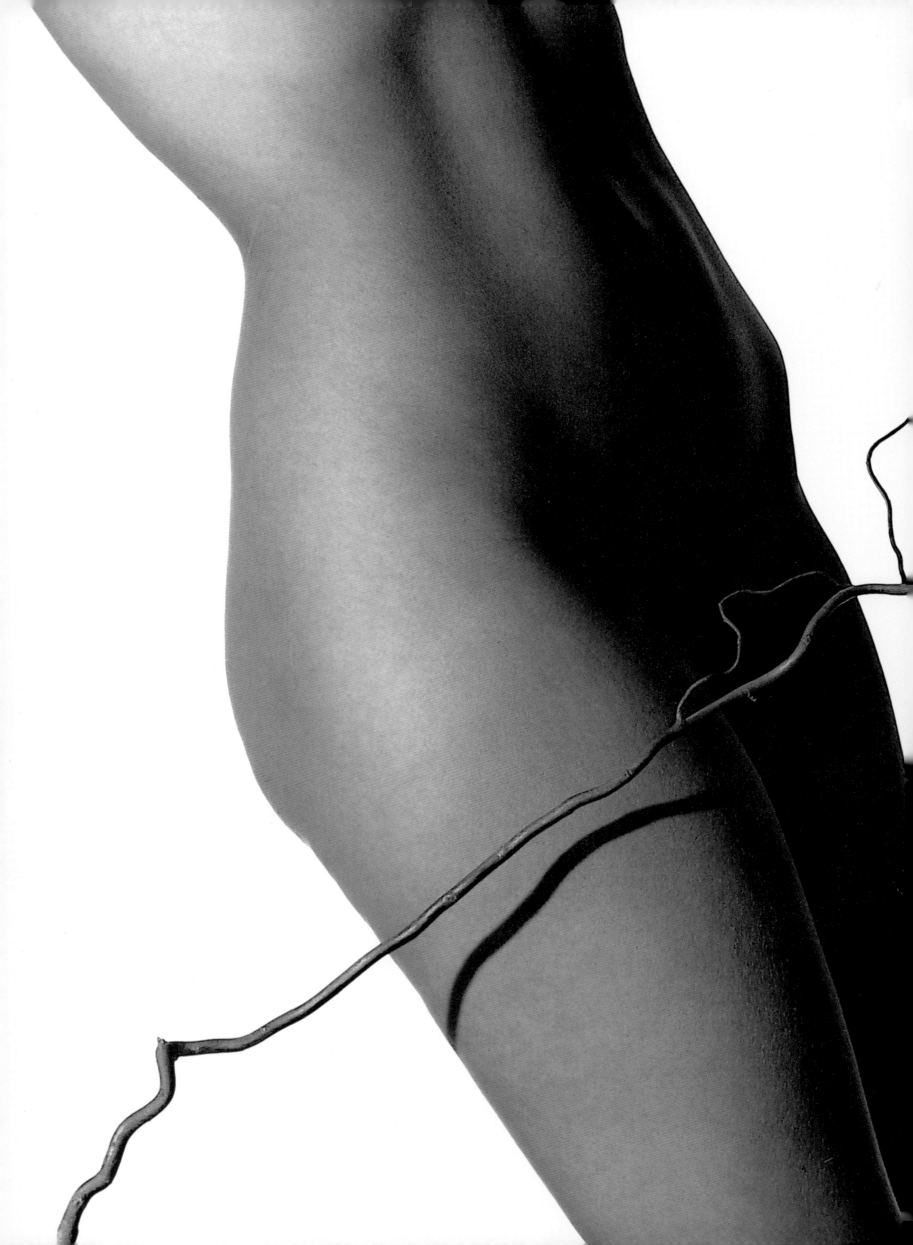

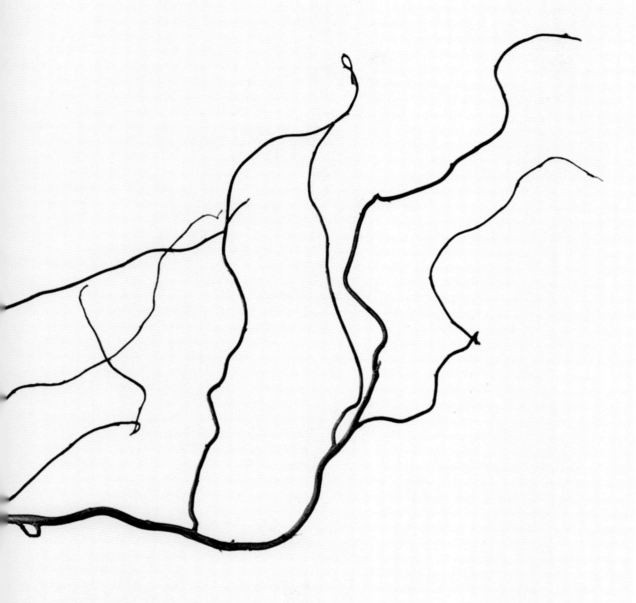

NUDE WITH TWIG 1991

MAYA ON CHAIR 1995

LA
ND
SCAPE

CORNWALL 1988

CUMBRIA 1988

ABU DHABI, THE UNITED ARAB EMIRATES   1992

ROCKY MOUNTAINS, CANADA   1986

NORFOLK 1991

KENYA 1991

CUMBRIA 1991

FARMHOUSE, DEVON 1990

AYERS ROCK, AUSTRALIA 1992

ARGYLL, SCOTLAND 1988

CUMBRIA 1989

UTAH, U.S.A. 1988
MAURITIUS 1993

ARGYLL, SCOTLAND 1990

CUMBRIA 1989

LONG ISLAND, NEW YORK   1983

GLENCOE, SCOTLAND   1991

CUMBRIA 1994

UTAH, U.S.A. 1988

ARGYLL, SCOTLAND 1990

PO RTRA ITS

SIR BOB GELDOF 1989

JACK VETTRIANO 1994
RIGHT: RUTH BERNHARD 1992

BRIAN CLARKE 1983
OVERLEAF: HELENA BONHAM-CARTER 1987

PETER LANGAN   1984
RIGHT: CHRIS COBIN AND JEREMY KING   1990

RICHARD BRANSON 1992

DAME JUDI DENCH 1988
OVERLEAF: DURAN DURAN 1986

SIR ROY STRONG 1990

ABOVE: JOAN COLLINS 1996
BRUCE OLDFIELD 1984
OVERLEAF: JAMES AND JULIA OGILVY 1993

ROBERT MAPPLETHORPE 1980
RIGHT: HORST P. HORST 1986

ANDY WARHOL 1979
OVERLEAF: JOHN PIPER 1977

SIR JOHN GIELGUD 1991
OVERLEAF: MARIANNE LAH–SWANNELL

JASPER CONRAN 1978
OVERLEAF: SIR ANDREW LLOYD-WEBBER 1983

TINA BROWN 1979
OVERLEAF: JACQUES-HENRI LARTIGUE 1977

ELTON JOHN 1989

MELVYN BRAGG 1992

HUGH JOHNSON 1981
RIGHT: BILLY CONNOLLY 1984

HELMUT NEWTON AND MARIE HELVIN 1977

PETE TOWNSHEND 1989

HRH THE PRINCESS ROYAL   1990

EVGENIA SANDS 1979
OVERLEAF: PETER BLAKE 1982

SIR DAVID PUTTNAM 1989

PALME D'OR ✦ CANNES 1986
MISSION
un film de
ROLAND JOFFÉ
JEREMY IRONS
MISSION
ÉCRIT PAR ROBERT BOLT
DAVID PUTTNAM

JANE SWANNELL 1990

ALICE SWANNELL 1980
RIGHT: MARIANNE, SOPHIA AND CHARLIE 1989

ACKNOWLEDGEMENTS

Olympus Cameras

Robert Mackintosh, my photographic assistant
Amber Webster, my personal assistant

Barry Taylor
David Bailey
Grant Scott
Sir Roy Strong
Jane Procter
Ian Dickens
Sir Bob Geldof
Karena Perronet-Miller
Mark Stenning
Malcolm Willison
David Burnham
Saul Henry
Robin Gibson
Terence Pepper
Mark Haworth-Booth
Brian Clarke
Martin Harrison
John Wingrove
Kathy Phillips
Anna Harvey
Naim Attallah
David Litchfield
Barbara & Laurence Tarlo
Andy Cowan
Tim Jeffries
Robin Bell
Bill Rawlinson
Pete Guest
Neil Palfreyman

All the fashion editors, make-up artists, hairdressers and model agencies
for their invaluable contributions